Dr. John King

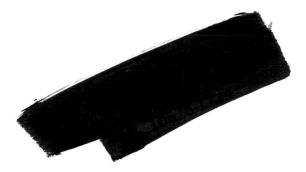

DILLON PRESS
New York

Picture acknowledgments

The Publisher would like to thank the following for providing illustrations for use in this book: John Frost 35 top; Billie Love 13; Christine Osborne 12, 16, 18 top; Photo Press 30 (A.Campbell); Popperfoto 11 (Katalin Arkell), 23 (AFP/FRAZZA), 29 (AFP), 35 bottom (AFP/B.Estrade), 44 (AFP/Nabil Ismail); Rex Features 37(Today), 38 (Sipa), 39 (Boccon-Gibod); Frank Spooner 4 (Pierre Perrin), 19 (F.Lochon), 33 bottom, 36 (Gilles Bassignac), 40 (Merillon/Chip Hires), 42 (Noel Quidu); Topham 5, 6, 7, 8, 10, 14, 17, 18 bottom, 20, 22, 24, 25, 26, 28, 31, 32, 33 top, 34.

The artwork on pages 9, 21, 27, and 41 is by Peter Bull.

Cover: Ahmadi oilfield, Kuwait. One of over 500 oil wells set on fire by retreating Iraqi forces during the Gulf War, in February 1991.

First American publication 1991 by Dillon Press,
Macmillan Publishing Company, 866 Third Avenue, New York, NY 10022

Macmillan Publishing Company is part of the Maxwell Communication Group of Companies.

First published in 1991 by Wayland (Publishers) Limited
61 Western Road, Hove, East Sussex BN3 1JD England

Printed in Scotland by Eagle Colourbooks Ltd.
10 9 8 7 6 5 4 3 2 1

Library of Congress Cataloging-in-Publication Data

King, John.
   The Gulf War / John King.
      p.   cm.
   Summary: Examines the causes, events, and aftermath of the recent
   conflict in the Persian Gulf.
   ISBN 0-87518-514-2
   1. Persian Gulf War. 1991 - - Juvenile literature. [1. Persian Gulf
   War. 1991.] I. Title
   DS79.72.K56   1991
   956.704'3--dc20

91-25744
CIP
AC

Contents

Invasion

At about 2:00 A.M. local time, on August 2, 1990, Iraqi tanks and troops swept over the border between Iraq and its southern neighbor, the small oil-rich state of Kuwait. Iraq's army was large, totaling a million men, against Kuwait's 17,000, and even a small advance guard easily overwhelmed Kuwait's defenses. The invasion, ordered by Iraqi President Saddam Hussein, began a confrontation that threatened the future of the entire Middle East region.

As Iraqi troops poured across the border, Kuwaiti radio broadcasts called upon Saddam Hussein to halt his offensive and settle his dispute with Kuwait without bloodshed. Alerted to the invasion by the U.S. embassy in Kuwait, the U.S. administration made an early statement condemning Iraq and calling for the immediate withdrawal of Iraqi forces. Britain added its voice, saying that Iraq was threatening the stability of the Middle East.

The Iraqis ignored these calls to halt and pressed onward. By morning they had taken control of Kuwait City, Kuwait's capital. Altogether 150,000 Iraqi troops entered Kuwait on the first day of the action; 30,000 of these occupied Kuwait City. The first hint many of the residents of Kuwait City had that the invasion had taken place was when they woke in the morning to find Iraqi tanks in the streets.

The ruler, or emir, of Kuwait, Prince Jaber al-Ahmed al-Sabah, together with the crown prince and heir to the throne, Prince Saad al-Abdullah al-Sabah, escaped capture during the night and fled to Saudi Arabia. From there, Prince Saad made a broadcast promising that Kuwait would fight on until its territory was regained. In Baghdad, the capital of Iraq, the news of the invasion was greeted with enthusiasm, and President Saddam Hussein's move was generally approved.

▲ *President Saddam Hussein of Iraq.*

Eyewitnesses were confused at first about what had happened. On the evening of August 2, the first day of the occupation, one Kuwaiti journalist described what he had seen and heard:

"When I looked out of my window I could see smoke billowing in the distance and could hear more machine-gun fire. We didn't realize what was going on until 6:00 A.M., when a statement was made by the Kuwaiti Defense Department. After that there was mass panic, with people calling their relatives to see if everything was all right. I went into the city at 10:00 A.M. Iraqi troops were manning all key government offices. Tanks were patrolling the city. The streets are now deserted and people are too frightened to go out." As the day wore on, foreigners living in Kuwait spoke of scenes of chaos and confusion,

▲ *The president of the United States, George Bush.*

with gunfire, explosions, and helicopters and jets overhead.

While Iraqi troops pushed southward toward the frontier between Kuwait and Saudi Arabia, brushing Kuwait's defenses aside, the Saudi authorities and the other Persian Gulf states maintained their silence. Kuwait was a member of the Gulf Cooperation Council (GCC), a political and military grouping in which Kuwait and Saudi Arabia were joined with Bahrain, Qatar, the United Arab Emirates (UAE), and Oman in what was meant to be a defensive alliance. The GCC, however, faced with its first real challenge, did nothing. The Arab states of the region were deeply shocked and very fearful as to what President Saddam Hussein might choose to do next.

On the first day after his invasion of Kuwait, President Saddam Hussein found himself facing worldwide disapproval. President George Bush made a statement claiming that there was "no place in today's world for this sort of naked aggression." The Soviet Union called for "the restoration of Kuwaiti sovereignty," and the Chinese government declared itself "extremely concerned," adding that no one should seek to solve problems by force of arms. The European Community condemned the action strongly, and Arab states including Algeria, Morocco, and Lebanon also spoke out against it. Only Jordan's King Hussein, in a hint of what his country's future attitude might be, called cautiously for the conflict to be "kept within an Arab framework."

Saddam Hussein's action against Kuwait found popular support in certain Arab states, in particular in Jordan, Sudan, and Yemen. In those countries many people saw the invasion as a blow against those few Arab states — such as Kuwait and Saudi Arabia — that were seen as monopolizing the oil profits that should be for the benefit of the whole Arab "nation." It was also seen as an act of defiance against the United States, which many Arabs blame for the plight of the Palestinians and for frustrating Arab achievements in other ways.

When the U.N. Security Council met on August 2, fourteen of its fifteen members voted for Resolution 660, which condemned Iraq's invasion of Kuwait and called for an immediate withdrawal, as well as negotiations between Iraq and Kuwait to resolve their differences. The Council's five permanent members are the United States, the Soviet Union, Britain, France, and China, and all five voted for the resolution in a demonstration of solidarity from both the West and the East. Only Yemen, the one Arab state holding a temporary Security Council seat in August 1990, abstained, and there were no votes against. The international community, with few exceptions, was firmly opposed to what Iraq had done.

U.N. Resolution 660 (August 2, 1990)

1. Condemns the Iraqi invasion of Kuwait.
2. Demands that Iraq withdraw immediately and unconditionally all its forces to the positions in which they were located on August 1, 1990.
3. Calls upon Iraq and Kuwait to begin immediately intensive negotiations for the resolution of their differences and supports all efforts in this regard, and especially those of the Arab League.

Why Invade Kuwait?

There had been friction between Iraq and Kuwait for some time, and during July 1990 the tension had mounted sharply. Some kind of action on Iraq's part had been half expected, but not on this scale. For example, an Iraqi occupation of the two offshore Kuwaiti islands of Bubiyan and Warbah, potentially of strategic use to Iraq, seemed possible. But behind Iraq's hostile attitude toward Kuwait was Iraq's need for funds. Iraq needed either to push up the price of oil or to acquire more oil resources. That is why a limited move by Iraq into part of northern Kuwait to seize some oil-producing areas seemed distinctly possible. But the full-scale occupation of Kuwait by Iraq was something else entirely, and no one outside Iraq had predicted it.

Motives

Saddam Hussein's aggressive style had long been a cause of apprehension for neighboring countries, and he was regarded with wary respect. In 1989 he had persuaded Egypt to join Yemen and Jordan in a regional grouping, the Arab Cooperation Council (ACC). The ACC was formed at Saddam Hussein's suggestion, and he intended to lead it.

Many observers of the Middle East have suggested that Saddam Hussein's ambition was to take on the mantle of President Gamal Abdel Nasser of Egypt. Until his death in 1970, Nasser was widely regarded as the leader of the Arab world, largely as a result of the Egyptian revolution of 1952 and his nationalization of the Suez Canal in 1956.

▲ *Kuwait's emir, Jaber al-Ahmed al-Sabah (center), with Crown Prince Saad al-Abdullah al-Sabah (left) at the emergency Arab summit meeting in Cairo, Egypt, on August 10, 1990.*

Arab leaders meeting in Iraq: From right to left, Yasser Arafat, chairman of the PLO, Saddam Hussein, King Hussein of Jordan, and the vice president of Yemen, Ali Salem al-Baidh. Some people have put forward the theory that there was a conspiracy among these leaders to divide up Kuwait and Saudi Arabia among themselves.

▼

Meanwhile Iraq and Kuwait had been on increasingly uneasy terms since the end of the 1980–1988 war between Iraq and Iran. The principal points of disagreement between the two countries were:

❑ There was an unresolved disagreement over the right to exploit certain oilfields, in particular the Rumailah oilfield, which straddles the Iraq–Kuwait border.

❑ There was a long-standing argument over the frontier between the two countries, which Iraq only briefly accepted after Kuwait's independence from British protection in 1961. In 1965 Iraq again challenged the legitimacy of the borders. The sovereignty of the Kuwaiti islands of Bubiyan and Warbah was also in dispute.

❑ Iraq claimed, with some justification, that Kuwait's high oil production was glutting the market and thus driving down the world price of oil. (With more oil for sale, all sellers are obliged to reduce their price to find purchasers for what they have produced, since only a limited amount of cash is available for the purchase of oil.)

❑ Kuwait wanted Iraq to repay the loans it had received during the Iran–Iraq war. Iraq wanted the debt canceled. In contrast to Kuwait, Saudi Arabia, which had also lent money to Iraq, made some of its loans into outright gifts. The Saudi Arabian government, led by King Fahd, had accepted Iraq's argument that the Iran–Iraq war had been fought to defend all Arab interests in the Persian Gulf against Iran.

In July 1990 the dispute between Iraq and Kuwait heated up. On July 17 President Saddam Hussein made a speech strongly attacking Kuwait for driving down the price of oil, which had fallen to $18 a barrel through over-production. The Iraqi government's efforts to get its economy back into shape after the costly Iran–Iraq war were being frustrated by the resulting loss of income. President Saddam Hussein alleged that Kuwait had deliberately produced more oil than the amount agreed upon by the Organization of Petroleum Exporting Countries (OPEC).

Saddam Hussein also accused Kuwait of "stealing" $2.4 billion worth of oil lifted by Kuwait from the Rumailah oilfield. The southern tip of the Rumailah field is in Kuwait, but Iraq alleged

that Kuwait's operations were reducing the level of the oilfield across its whole area, including the part that lies inside Iraq. These accusations were accompanied by a direct demand from Iraqi Foreign Minister Tarek Aziz that Kuwait should cancel all the debts incurred by Iraq during its war with Iran.

Kuwait rejected Iraq's accusations. On July 20 the Arab League and Saudi Arabia offered their services as mediators between Iraq and Kuwait, in what was beginning to look like a potentially dangerous dispute. That was followed by a rapid round of diplomatic talks led by President Mubarak of Egypt and King Hussein of Jordan to reconcile the dispute between Iraq and Kuwait. At the same time the Iraqi government stepped up its threats against Kuwait, and more Iraqi troops were moved up to the frontier with Kuwait. A few days before the invasion, the Iraqi force on the Kuwaiti border was reported to have reached an estimated 100,000 men, with 300 tanks.

On July 27 at its meeting in Geneva, OPEC made its own contribution to the attempt to negotiate with the Iraqi government by raising the official oil price from $18 to $21 a barrel. After much persuasion by the Egyptian and Jordanian leaders, an Iraqi delegation led by Saddam Hussein's deputy, Izzat Ibrahim, the vice president of Iraq's ruling Revolutionary Command Council, met Kuwaiti representatives in the Saudi Arabian city of Jeddah on July 31. However, little progress was made toward settling the dispute, and the meeting was abandoned the following day.

Iraq claimed that Kuwait was refusing to take its complaints seriously and that Kuwait was acting "against Iraq's basic interests." Kuwait's delegation to the talks was led by Crown Prince Saad al-Abdullah al-Sabah, who issued a statement saying he wanted to continue talks with Iraq.

But for President Saddam Hussein it was too late for talks. He now made the decision to order the invasion of Kuwait, and his army units were in place on the frontier ready to move forward.

◀ *The former U.S. ambassador to Iraq, April Glaspie. Did she inadvertently encourage Saddam Hussein?*

The Wrong Message

It could be argued that Saddam Hussein was not altogether mistaken in believing that the United States was encouraging him to strengthen his position as Iraqi leader and rebuild his country after the Iran–Iraq war. A conversation on July 25 between Saddam Hussein and the U.S. ambassador to Iraq, April Glaspie, is said to have given Saddam Hussein encouragement, by leading him to believe that the United States would not object to an Iraqi move against Kuwait. The Iraqis released the following transcript of the conversation:

Saddam Hussein: The price of oil at one stage had dropped to $12 a barrel, and a reduction in the modest Iraqi budget of $6–7 billion is a disaster.

April Glaspie: I think I understand this. I have lived here for years. I admire your extraordinary efforts to rebuild your country. I know you need funds. We understand that, and our opinion is that you should have the opportunity to rebuild your country. But we have no opinion on Arab – Arab conflicts like your border disagreement with Kuwait.

April Glaspie later claimed that she actually added something to the effect that military intervention would run counter to U.S. wishes. Saddam Hussein seems to have overestimated the U.S. government's reluctance to become involved in the dispute. He may have believed that if the United States were willing to stand aside, the world would not act against him.

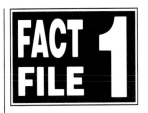

Geography

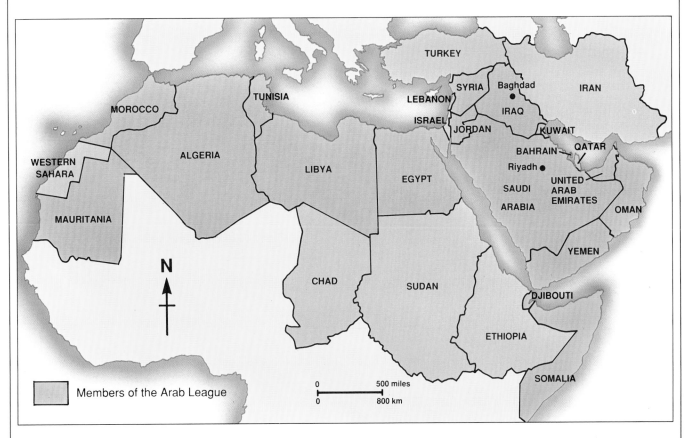

Members of the Arab League

0   500 miles
0   800 km

▲ *The PLO is also a member of the Arab League. See the map on page 27.*

The Arab World

Iraq and Kuwait lie adjacent to each other on the eastern fringe of the Arab world, of which they are both part. Arab lands stretch from Morocco's Atlantic coast in the west to Oman at the mouth of the Persian Gulf in the east. The northernmost Arab territory is in the north of Syria and Iraq, bordering on Turkey, while to the south, in Africa, Sudan is a largely Arab country, and Mauritania is a member of the Arab Maghreb Union. Twenty Arab states, together with Palestine, are members of the Arab League, the international political body to which Arab countries all adhere, and the number of people who regard themselves as Arabs is approaching 200 million.

Arabs range from the black Sudanese to light-skinned northern peoples. The common thread in Arab countries is not ethnic but linguistic. The Arabic language, which is the same across the whole Arab world in its written form, though spoken dialects differ, binds Arabs powerfully into a cultural unity. Music, poetry, and a common tradition are shared and enjoyed everywhere in Arab countries. Most Arabs are Muslims, but there are also substantial Christian minorities of many different denominations. While the right of Christians to regard themselves as Arabs is not in dispute, Islam and the Koran provide the strongest common cultural element throughout the Arab countries.

Adjacent to the Arab lands in the east are countries that, though Muslim, are separated from the Arabs by language. Though Turkey

9

and Iran, which border Iraq to the north and east, share the religion of Islam, "true" Arabs regard the people of those countries as foreigners in a way in which even Arabs from widely separated Arab states never think of each other. Iran is the heartland of Shi'ite Islam, a school separate from the normal Arab Sunni Islam, the orthodox version of the faith. The Arabs of Africa are also sharply differentiated from their more southerly African neighbors, even where the dividing line runs across a country, as it does in Sudan and Chad.

Arab Neighbors

Though Iraq and Kuwait are Arab neighbors, they are also very different. The people of Kuwait are very like those of southern Iraq in their speech and manners. But Iraq is a large and varied country, with a population of 18 million, while Kuwait had only 2 million

inhabitants before the Gulf War, of whom less than a million were Kuwaiti citizens. Iraq is a large country, covering 170,000 square miles, while Kuwait occupies only a little less than 7,000 square miles, just over a twenty-fifth of Iraq's area. Kuwait has a coastline and an open port, while Iraq's access to the Gulf is restricted to 25 miles of the marshy coastline at the mouth of the Shatt el-Arab waterway.

But the crucial difference between the two countries is wealth. Both have large oil resources (each contains almost 10 percent of the world's oil reserves), but Kuwait exists on oil, and its large resources and small population mean that before the Gulf War the Kuwaiti people lived very well.

Kuwait: The Oil Oasis

Oil has yielded Kuwait an enormous income. Before the Gulf crisis, Kuwait produced

Kuwait City before the crisis: A picture of affluence. ▼

Visible wealth: The gold market in Kuwait City. ▶

one and a half million barrels of oil a day — that is, about a quarter of a million tons. That money has been carefully invested. Before the Gulf War the $100 billion of Kuwaiti investments overseas, controlled by the Kuwait Investment Organization, produced at least $6 billion a year in income. This figure is comparable to the amount of money Kuwait makes each year from selling oil.

Oil has transformed Kuwait into a wealthy society. Its gross national product, or GNP (the total value of all the goods and services provided by a country, which gives a measure of national income), was over $26 billion in 1989. That means Kuwait enjoyed a GNP per head of the population of $13,000, which makes it one of the world's richest countries. Even this figure does not represent the real wealth of Kuwait's people, since many of the foreign workers, who made up half of Kuwait's prewar population, were low-paid servants or laborers from countries such as the Philippines and Sri Lanka. The effective GNP per head of Kuwait's own citizens was even higher.

Kuwait City had become a capital city of great wealth. The houses of rich Kuwaitis were extremely luxurious, and even ordinary Kuwaitis lived in great comfort. Banks and supermarkets were air-conditioned (a great advantage in the desert heat) and were overflowing with goods and services. Cars were new and plentiful. New construction was on an ambitious scale. The welfare of Kuwait's citizens was well looked after by the state, with good education and health services. Kuwait City was the main population center, and outside the city and its expanding suburbs were the oil wells, other oil installations, and some smaller settlements associated with the oil industry.

On the other hand, Kuwait before the war was a society ridden with class distinctions. The thousand or so members of the ruling al-Sabah family effectively controlled the country. The country's 1962 constitution, which guaranteed at least a limited democracy, had been suspended by the emir, Prince Jaber al-Ahmed al-Sabah, in 1985. This was after repeated political upheavals in the National Assembly, leading to the resignation of the government on the grounds that it could no longer carry on its work in the face of opposition criticism. Kuwaiti citizens were divided into first and second classes. "First-class citizens" were those whose direct male ancestors were residents before 1920, and only "first-class" males had voting rights. "Second-class citizens" were residents whose families had not acquired Kuwaiti nationality before 1920.

Most Kuwaitis are Sunni Muslims, professing the orthodox view of the faith followed by most Arabs, but a quarter, including even some of the oldest families, are Shi'ites, with historic connections with Iran.

There were also expatriates of various Arab and non-Arab origins, some wealthy and others who were earning relatively small sums. Palestinians, some with Jordanian nationality, held many professional posts before the crisis, and there were also numerous Palestinian merchants and traders, as well as other workers. Jordanians, Egyptians, Sudanese, Iraqis, and other Arab nationals did work of all kinds, from doctors and lawyers to laborers and servants. Many domestic servants came from the Philippines or Sri Lanka, and there was a large group of Bangladeshi, Indian, and Pakistani workers, as well as workers from other developing countries. Finally, there were many expatriates from Western countries, most doing technical or managerial jobs.

Iraq: Squandered Resources

Although Iraq has large oil resources and actually exported more oil than Kuwait (2.5 million barrels a day) before the crisis, it was and is a poorer country. For thousands of years Iraq has been an agricultural country, watered by the Tigris and Euphrates rivers, but there is now a substantial amount of industry, into which the Iraqi regime has put a significant investment. In fact, Iraq's oil revenue could have transformed the country, but a great deal of the money was spent on armaments during the exhausting eight-year war with Iran, which caused Iraq to run up at least $65 billion of international debt. Iraq's GNP is not officially declared, but the World Bank regards it as an upper-middle-income country, on a par with Malaysia and Argentina, which implies that Iraq has an income per head of some $3,000. That figure is backed up by other studies. Even after trade sanctions were applied to Iraq in August 1990, Iraqis never went hungry or lacked the basic necessities.

Few Iraqis are very rich, and poverty in Iraq has in the past seldom been extreme. Iraq is a country divided not so much into social classes as into geographical segments. The people in the south of Iraq are Shi'ite Muslims, who share their religion with neighboring Iran. The Shi'ites make up 55 percent of Iraq's population. In the north are the Kurds, a quarter of Iraq's population, who are mainly Sunni Muslims, though there are also some Shi'ite Kurds. The Kurds speak a separate language of their own, related to Farsi, the language of Iran, while a handful of Iraqi nationals are Farsi or Turkish speakers. There is a significant Christian minority of 5 percent. Most Iraqi Christians follow the Chaldean rite, though other churches are represented. Iraqi society has been changed by Saddam Hussein and the Baath party of which he is a member — a transformation that is discussed in the next two chapters.

▲ *Iraq's capital, Baghdad, and the Tigris.*

History

The Ottoman Empire

Until World War I (1914–1918), Iraq and Kuwait were both part of the Ottoman Empire, the historic Turkish state ruled from Istanbul, which had dominated the Middle East for many centuries. The region that is now the modern state of Iraq was added to the Ottoman possessions by the Ottoman Sultan Suleiman the Magnificent in the sixteenth century. Modern Iraq is composed of three provinces originally set out by the Turks: Baghdad, Mosul in the north, and Basra in the south. In the late nineteenth century the Turks extended their authority into the Arabian peninsula, adding the coastal regions of the Gulf and areas of what is now Saudi Arabia to the province of Basra.

Kuwait first became a part of the Ottoman Empire in 1871, and that provided one of the justifications for Iraq's claim that Kuwait is lawfully a part of Iraq that was separated by the later activities of colonial administrators. There is some justice in that claim, but Kuwait had already been ruled by the al-Sabah family, the modern ruling family, for 150 years by the time it was incorporated (voluntarily) into the Ottoman Empire, while the ruler was given a special Ottoman title as governor. So, in a sense, Kuwait always had a separate existence.

British Intervention

During the late nineteenth century the British government was developing an early interest in

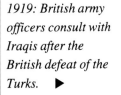

1919: British army officers consult with Iraqis after the British defeat of the Turks. ▶

Iraq and the Gulf. The region was one of the staging posts on the way to India (then part of the British Empire), and the British began to open up Iraq and the Gulf coast for trade. A regular steamship service was inaugurated between Basra and Bombay in 1862, and British Indian postal services were extended to Basra for the benefit of traders. But it was in Kuwait that British protection began to appeal to the al-Sabah family, who saw an opportunity to break free from the Turks.

In 1899 the Kuwaiti ruler Sheikh Mubarak signed an agreement with Britain insuring his protection, and in 1913, with British help, borders were defined between Kuwait, the Arabian region known as Nejd, and the province of Basra. At this stage, a theoretical Turkish sovereignty over Kuwait was still recognized, though in practice it was Britain that was in control.

The End of Turkish Rule
During World War I, when the Ottomans allied themselves with the Germans, Kuwait and the

◀ *Kuwait's oil industry gets into gear: A new oil refinery comes on stream in 1958.*

people of the Nejd region declared themselves to be on the side of the British, and in 1914 Britain promised the ruler of Kuwait that it would become an independent Arab state, or emirate, under British protection.

When the Turks were defeated, Britain and France — now the dominant states in both the Arabian Peninsula and the more northerly Arab lands — divided up the former Turkish possessions between them. The story of the Arab revolt, linked with the name of Lawrence of Arabia, is well known. Colonel Lawrence, a British army officer, helped to organize the revolt of Arabs against Turkish rule. He gave encouragement to the Hashemite family of the Hejaz, Sherif Hussein of Mecca and his sons, to rise up against the Turks.

The Cairo Conference

Decisions on the shape of the Middle East after the fall of the Ottoman Empire were made at the Cairo Conference of 1921, where Winston Churchill, as British colonial secretary, presided over the future of the region. The boundaries of modern Iraq, which includes the Kurdish region in the north and the Shi'ite south, as well as the central region previously ruled from Baghdad, were set. If there is a claim that Kuwait was an artificial colonial creation, it should also be remembered that the boundaries of modern Iraq were created at this time.

Britain and Kuwait

Meanwhile, Kuwait had fought off a challenge to its independence in 1920 from Ibn Saud, the sultan of Nejd, who later became the founder of Saudi Arabia. In 1922 Sir Percy Cox, the British high commissioner in Iraq, moved to end the boundary dispute by calling a conference, bringing together the rulers of Kuwait and Iraq with Ibn Saud. Cox defined the boundaries between the states, giving Iraq much northern territory that Ibn Saud would have liked to control, but handing over to the Saudis part of the area claimed by Kuwait. Kuwait itself became the object of formal British protection, and the boundaries in the region were finally defined in 1923, to be confirmed in 1932, when Iraq became independent.

Britain's interest in Kuwait in the twentieth century was focused on the supply of oil. Britain's colonial possessions did not include a source of oil, and it was already recognized that oil was the fuel of the future. There seemed a possibility that oil would be found in Kuwait, and part of the relationship between Britain and Kuwait was an agreement that only Britain would be allowed to exploit Kuwaiti oil. That was a source of annoyance to the United States, which reacted by initiating a search for oil in Saudi Arabia that was very fruitful in due course.

Britain maintained its special relationship with Kuwait throughout World War II and the postwar period. Postwar Iraq was guided by the pro-Western statesman Nuri el-Said, and Iraq joined Britain in the Baghdad Pact, an arrangement for mutual defense designed to exclude Soviet influence from the region. But in 1958 the Iraqi monarchy was overthrown by a military *coup d'état*, the first of many, and Nuri and the young King Faisal II were killed. In spite of the unsettled state of the region, Britain proceeded to give Kuwait full sovereignty in 1961.

Iraq Claims Kuwait

General Qassem, who took power in Iraq in 1958, asserted Iraq's historic claim to sovereignty over Kuwait in 1961, after the British had left. By 1963 Iraq looked likely to pose a serious military challenge to Kuwait.

British troops moved back in to defend Kuwait's frontiers. Kuwait's security was assured, and Iraq agreed to respect Kuwait's borders, but the Iraqi claim was asserted again in 1965. The Baathists in Iraq have never accepted Kuwait's frontiers, and they have also never wholly abandoned the claim reasserted by President Saddam Hussein that Iraq has a historic right to Kuwait based on the Ottoman sovereignty over it. In the 1970s and 1980s Kuwait remained close to the West as its oil wealth grew to enormous proportions. Kuwait maintained special financial links with Great

▲ *Bedouin children and tents in the Kuwaiti desert — second-class Kuwaitis?*

Britain and with the United States, one of Kuwait's oil customers.

Modern Kuwait

The power and wealth of the ruling family have meant that Kuwait has been run as a family business. The suspension of the constitution in 1985 nevertheless gave rise to discontent in a country much used to debate and dissent – in spite of the ruling family's power. There are outspoken opponents to the al-Sabah government, but when Kuwait was invaded in August 1990, the country was, in effect, an autocracy headed by a traditional ruler. Its social structure gave some justification to one of President Saddam Hussein's claims, that he was asserting natural justice by taking property from the "haves" of the Arab world and redistributing it to the "have-nots." It may be possible that Saddam Hussein thought that he might receive support for the invasion from Kuwait's less wealthy citizens.

Hussein's Iraq

Saddam Hussein was born in 1937 in Takrit, in the countryside about 90 miles north of Baghdad. He had a hard childhood and was brought up in a poor village by a stepfather, and later by an uncle, who took him to Baghdad. There are many stories about the harshness of Saddam Hussein's upbringing, his solitary nature, his cruelty, and his ambitions, but it is difficult to know how many of these stories to believe, since many of them are told by his enemies.

As a twenty-year-old student in 1957, Saddam Hussein became a member of the Baath ("Rebirth") party (see below). The coup in July 1958, in which King Faisal II was killed, opened the way for the Baath and for Saddam Hussein. In 1959 he took part in a failed attempt on the life of the Iraqi Republic's first president, General Qassem, seen by the Baath as an obstacle to their gaining power. Saddam Hussein fled to Syria, where he made contact with the Syrian Baathists, and then went to Cairo, where he became a law student.

The New Iraq

After the 1958 coup the new leaders were self-styled Free Officers, whose movement was a conscious imitation of the Egyptian group led by Egypt's President Nasser in the 1950s and 1960s. The officers' regime in Iraq was anti-Western and pro-Egyptian.

Qassem's regime lasted until 1963, when he was overthrown and executed by his former colleague Abdel Salaam Aref, who had helped with the 1958 coup. On this occasion, the new rulers called themselves Nasserists and Baathists, and it was now that the Baath party entered Iraqi politics for the first time, enabling the exiled Saddam Hussein to return to the country. Aref temporarily ousted the Baath faction, but he died in an air crash in 1966. He was succeeded by his brother Abderrahman Aref. In 1968 another member of the Free Officers group, Ahmed Hassan Bakr, a cousin of Saddam Hussein's uncle, toppled Abderrahman Aref, and the Baath took power.

The Baath Party

The Baath was a political party founded in the idealistic philosophy of a Syrian Christian, Michel Aflaq. The slogans of the Baath, which means "rebirth," were "Unity, Freedom, Socialism," and "One Arab Nation with an Eternal Mission." The redistribution of wealth and land was part of the Baath's program, together with a strong belief in the need to unify the Arab people. For the Baath, frontiers between Arab states were a creation of colonialists, Turkish or Western,

President Nasser of Egypt, for two decades the Arab world's charismatic hero, pictured here on the cover of Time *magazine.* ▶

القائد المناضل صدام حسين

and the Arabs were intended to become one nation. In the hands of the officers of Iraq's army, the Baathist philosophy later became a justification for extreme actions. Harsh deeds were always pardonable if they were deemed necessary to help achieve the Arab revolution.

The Rise of Saddam Hussein

From the early 1970s Saddam Hussein was an active member of Bakr's administration, gradually taking more of the reins of power into his own hands. Saddam Hussein put his own relatives and friends into key positions, until he was effectively in control of the country and the armed forces. He likes to wear military uniforms, but he has never been a soldier. He always keeps the armed forces under his close control. From the beginning, one of the ways in which Saddam Hussein asserted himself was through his control of the security services.

In 1979 Bakr resigned his posts and Saddam Hussein took over as president, giving formal recognition to the control Saddam Hussein had already achieved. Since then President Saddam

Hussein has been careful to maintain his hold on power. He has often been accused of eliminating opponents and even potential opponents, and he has always taken steps to suppress dissent from Iraq's minority

Iraq's first president, General Qassem (right), with Colonel Abdel Salaam Aref. ▼

communities, the Kurds and the Shi'ites. He has made a ruling class out of the people he grew up with in the region of Takrit. His relatives and childhood acquaintances have been promoted within the Baath party and appointed to influential positions.

In 1980 President Saddam Hussein began the war against Iran, which was to last for eight years. Iran looked weak, just a year after the Islamic revolution. He hoped to gain control over the waterway to the Gulf (the Shatt el-Arab) shared between the two countries, and perhaps to annex oil-producing areas in south-western Iran. The losses of the eight years of war were enormous on both sides, and its results inconclusive. After his invasion of Kuwait in 1990, Saddam Hussein reached an agreement with the Iranians that nullified any gains he might have made during the war. Nevertheless, the Iran–Iraq war enabled him to claim he was a defender of the whole Arab nation and also to gain support from the West. The United States was eager to support any

attack on Iran's Islamic republic, which it saw as a menace to political stability in the Gulf region. And while Saddam Hussein maintained and even built up the link between Iraq and the Soviet Union, which had been a principal arms supplier, he also built links with the West. Iraq bought arms from around the world with the money lent to it by the Gulf states and with oil revenues, but one of the main Western suppliers was France.

In the postwar period, after the cease-fire with Iran was declared in 1988, Saddam Hussein tried to build up his position as a potential leader of the Arab world. The Arab Cooperation Council (ACC), which involved Yemen, Jordan, and Egypt in a group meant to promote trade and military cooperation, was one vehicle. But as we have seen, Iraq needed money to recover from the efforts of the Iran–Iraq war, and in the end Saddam Hussein probably felt that the annexation of Kuwait, if he could carry it out unchallenged, would solve the economic crisis that Iraq was facing.

FACT FILE 4 Oil

Many commentators on the Gulf War have pointed out the importance of oil. Would the United States have acted to save Kuwait if it did not have such massive oil reserves? President Bush spoke about the intolerable nature of the invasion and the breach of international law. But on other occasions elsewhere in the world similar acts have gone unchallenged. Examples of these are China's invasion and occupation of Tibet (which became an autonomous region of China in 1965) and Indonesia's annexation of East Timor in 1976. Concerning the postwar situation in the Gulf, the government of the United States has now become more open about acknowledging its own aims. The assured supply of oil at a "reasonable price" certainly appeared to be one of the strategic aims of the U.S. administration.

The Gulf, including Iraq and Iran, is the world's largest and most vital source of oil. Oil is an irreplaceable resource, and 64 percent of the world's known oil reserves are concentrated in Iraq, Iran, and the six Gulf states, namely Kuwait, Bahrain, Qatar, the United Arab Emirates, Oman, and Saudi Arabia (see table next page). By comparison, the Soviet Union has less than 6 percent of the world's oil, and the United States has just over 3 percent.

The Gulf states, Iraq, and Iran are members of the Organization of Petroleum Exporting Countries (OPEC). OPEC also includes Algeria and Libya in the North African region, as well as Nigeria and Gabon from sub-Saharan Africa, Venezuela and Ecuador from the group of Latin American oil-producing countries, and a major Far Eastern producer, Indonesia. OPEC controls a large proportion of the world's oil reserves and production, and it acts to control prices by fixing the amount of oil each country produces.

▲ *Kuwait's lifeblood: Pipelines feeding oil out to waiting tankers.*

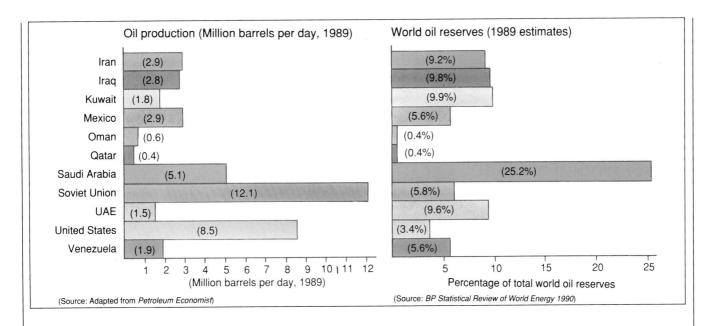

Oil production (Million barrels per day, 1989)

Country	Million barrels per day
Iran	(2.9)
Iraq	(2.8)
Kuwait	(1.8)
Mexico	(2.9)
Oman	(0.6)
Qatar	(0.4)
Saudi Arabia	(5.1)
Soviet Union	(12.1)
UAE	(1.5)
United States	(8.5)
Venezuela	(1.9)

(Million barrels per day, 1989)

(Source: Adapted from *Petroleum Economist*)

World oil reserves (1989 estimates)

Country	Percentage of total world oil reserves
Iran	(9.2%)
Iraq	(9.8%)
Kuwait	(9.9%)
Mexico	(5.6%)
Oman	(0.4%)
Qatar	(0.4%)
Saudi Arabia	(25.2%)
Soviet Union	(5.8%)
UAE	(9.6%)
United States	(3.4%)
Venezuela	(5.6%)

Percentage of total world oil reserves

(Source: *BP Statistical Review of World Energy 1990*)

▲ *Countries such as the Soviet Union and the United States are producing large quantities of oil at present, but they may ultimately come to rely on Gulf oil reserves.*

OPEC provides about a quarter of U.S. oil needs. Only 7 percent of America's oil comes from Saudi Arabia and 1 percent came from Kuwait before the Iraqi invasion. OPEC was a more important source of supply for Western Europe, which took half its oil from OPEC countries, and Japan, which took more than half its needs from OPEC. Something approaching 10 percent of Japan's oil came from Kuwait, as did around 5 percent of Europe's needs. So it was easy enough for the United States to replace the lost supply of oil from Kuwait. And, in any case, Saudi Arabia easily expanded its production to fill the gap.

In light of all these figures, it is easy to see that the actual loss of Kuwait's oil was not so important in the short term to the United States. But it is to the future that the United States is looking when it tries to secure oil resources. Its own reserves amount to only 34 billion barrels of oil; if the United States used only its own oil, with a rate of consumption of 16 million barrels a day, it could use up its oil resources in just six years. At its present rate of usage, it would run out of domestically produced oil soon after the year 2000. Gulf oil will become increasingly important to the United States and looks like it will be able to provide for the country's needs and those of the rest of the industrialized world for a century or so, if fuel is used economically

and other sources of energy become available.

As the United States has become more dependent on imported oil resources, American politicians have become anxious to keep the control of oil out of hostile hands, such as those of President Saddam Hussein. In that situation, the price of oil could be forced up and the economies of the industrialized countries could collapse under the strain of increasingly expensive fuel. There is an argument, however, that because oil producers need to sell their oil, if the Western economies did collapse the Gulf states would lose their best customers. They cannot, as is often said, drink oil. And that should insure a reasonable price.

On the other hand, a monopoly over the world's principal oil reserve would still put someone with President Saddam Hussein's political skills in a very powerful position. If he were allowed to keep Kuwait, he would be a permanent menace to Saudi Arabia and its oil reserves.

All these circumstances make it clear that the leaders of the United States, the other Western countries, and even the Soviet Union and China must have had the future of oil on their minds when deciding how to respond to Iraq's invasion of Kuwait. Without a doubt, the need to secure oil supplies will also affect how the crisis in the Gulf is finally resolved.

The Crisis Begins

August

Invasion Condemned

On August 3 governments around the world began to issue statements condemning Iraq's invasion, and they began to freeze Iraq's assets and suspend its international trade. The European Community collectively condemned the invasion, and in Cairo the Arab League issued a statement calling for immediate and unconditional withdrawal of Iraq's forces. Jordan, Libya, Yemen, Sudan, Djibouti, and the Palestinian Liberation Organization (PLO) refused to endorse the call, and of course Iraq itself held out against the Arab League's majority decision. The split at the Arab League reflected the division between those Arab states that supported the American-led alliance against Iraq, and those who expressed some degree of sympathy for Saddam Hussein's case.

A Gulf Cooperation Council meeting in Cairo and a meeting of the Islamic Conference Organization, an international body of which Arab and non-Arab Muslim states are members, both called for Iraq's withdrawal. The U.S. government was already beginning, on the first full day after the invasion, to bring pressure on King Fahd of Saudi Arabia to allow U.S. troops into the country to deter Iraq from invading. The U.S. administration stated that it was concerned because Iraqi troops were so close to the Saudi frontier, and President Bush warned Saddam Hussein about attacking Saudi Arabia itself. In the weeks that followed, rumors were rife in the Arab world that there was a conspiracy involving Jordan and Yemen, which would join Iraq in dismembering Saudi Arabia.

Pro-Iraqi Government in Kuwait?

In Kuwait, meanwhile, the formation of a so-called "transitional free government" was

▲ *U.S. commanders at the front, in Saudi Arabia, brief Richard Cheney, U.S. defense secretary (center).*

proclaimed on August 2, and on August 3 Iraq announced the deposition of the emir and the confiscation of the ruling family's assets. Saddam Hussein hoped to set up antiroyalist Kuwaitis in an administration that would favor Iraq. But no Kuwaitis were ever found who would lend their names to the scheme. The names of a cabinet allegedly composed of Kuwaiti officers was announced on August 4, but Kuwaiti diplomats outside the country said the ministers appointed were all Iraqi officers.

Advice for Saddam Hussein

King Hussein of Jordan flew to Baghdad on August 3 for a discussion with Saddam Hussein, probably to warn him to be cautious. On August 8 King Hussein made a televised plea for an Arab solution — without the involvement of foreign forces — to what he called an "Arab problem." At the same time the chairman of the PLO, Yasser Arafat, met the Libyan leader Colonel Gaddafi to agree on a peace plan aimed at avoiding Western intervention in the Gulf. Arafat went to Baghdad the following day to present his plan to Saddam Hussein.

U.N. Response: Sanctions

On August 6 the U.N .Security Council passed Resolution 661 (Yemen and Cuba abstained), which effectively imposed a tough trade embargo on Iraq. This then formed the basis of the U.N. sanctions that isolated Iraq from all foreign trade, depriving it of the oil revenue on which it depended and cutting it off from the import of goods and food.

August 10: The U.N. Security Council votes unanimously in favor of Resolution 662, declaring Iraq's annexation of Kuwait "null and void." ▼

U.S. Troops Sent In

By August 8 President Bush had prevailed over King Fahd's caution, and the first U.S. troops were arriving in Saudi Arabia, as President Bush addressed the American people on television. President Bush claimed there

were four principles behind America's action:
❏ to bring about the withdrawal of Iraq forces;
❏ to restore Kuwait's former government;
❏ to protect the stability of the Gulf region;
❏ to protect American citizens in the Gulf region.

Kuwait Annexed

Also on August 8 President Saddam Hussein abandoned the attempt to set up a pro-Iraqi government in Kuwait and announced the annexation of Kuwait by Iraq.

August 10

❏ Iraq's annexation of Kuwait was unanimously condemned in U.N. Security Council Resolution 662.
❏ An Arab League emergency summit meeting was held in Cairo. The meeting was attended by all the Arab states except Tunisia. President Saddam Hussein sent a delegation to represent Iraq, and the emir of Kuwait was present. The meeting discussed a motion refusing to

recognize Iraq's annexation of Kuwait and authorizing the dispatch of Arab forces to help Saudi Arabia. The motion was carried, with twelve states voting in favor. Iraq, Libya, and the PLO voted against, while Algeria and Yemen abstained. Jordan, Sudan, and Mauritania expressed reservations and refused to give a positive vote.

❑ President Saddam Hussein made a televised speech in Baghdad launching a blistering attack on the oil-rich Arab states and the United States. He called on Arabs and Muslims everywhere to join forces to repel what he called the American invaders, and he attempted to appeal to Muslim religious sentiments, calling for a *"jihad,"* or "holy war." Throughout the Arab world, there was much popular support for President Saddam Hussein and his move against Kuwait. There was also support for Iraq's action in Muslim countries outside the Arab world, including Pakistan.

Allies Send Troops In

The members of the Arab League who had voted for an Arab force to protect Saudi Arabia soon began to implement their decision. Egyptian troops arrived in Saudi Arabia on August 11. And troops from Europe, including Britain, began to move. The first British aircraft left Britain for the Gulf on August 11.

Saddam Hussein's Peace Plan

On August 12 Saddam Hussein announced his own plan for peace, calling for the withdrawal of American forces from Saudi Arabia, their replacement by Arab forces, and an end to the economic sanctions imposed on Iraq. He also called for Syrian troops to leave Lebanon, and for Israel to withdraw from the Occupied Territories (see glossary).

On the following day, King Hussein of Jordan appeared on Jordanian television to condemn the build-up of Western troops in Arab lands. King Hussein said that, in his view, the Western interest was more to protect oil supplies than to help the peoples of the Middle East.

August 15

Saddam Hussein agreed to all the demands made by Iran at the time of the cease-fire in the Iran–Iraq war two years earlier, in order to achieve peace with his eastern neighbor. The move meant, in effect, that Iraq had won nothing in return for eight years of war.

August 18

The speaker of Iraq's parliament made the announcement that Iraq would be the "host" of foreign citizens who had been in Iraq and Kuwait when the crisis began. Though women and children were soon freed and started to leave Iraq on September 1, the idea was to hold foreigners at "military bases and key civilian installations" as a "human shield" against attack. Iraqi troops had already begun rounding up Westerners in Kuwait. Other foreign workers in Kuwait, such as Egyptians, Indians, and Bangladeshis, continued to flee Kuwait, through Iraq and into Jordan, trying to get back to their home countries.

August 28

In a presidential decree, Iraq declared Kuwait to be Iraq's nineteenth province.

▲ *Asian refugees rest in a crowded shelter in the Jordanian capital, Amman, after fleeing from Kuwait.*

THE GULF WAR

Months of Tension

September and October

September and October were a period of diplomacy and negotiation, when it still seemed as if the sanctions applied by the U.N. to Iraq might bring President Saddam Hussein to accept that Iraq could not continue to defy the world. U.N. Resolution 665, passed on August 25, allowed the use of force to halt ships suspected of trading with Iraq. After that, Iraq was effectively cut off from all trade. If the sanctions could seriously affect Iraq's economy, it was hoped that they might be enough to force President Saddam Hussein to back down.

Military Build-up

By the end of September U.S. military intelligence was estimating that there were at least 300,000 Iraqi troops in Kuwait and the Iraqi frontier zone. Meanwhile the alliance ranged against Iraq was building up its forces in Operation Desert Shield, as the action was

known, in Saudi Arabia. By the beginning of October allied troops totaled around 250,000, including 200,000 Americans. At this stage, however, the allied commanders felt that they were not strong enough to mount an attack, and the aim of the troops seemed to be to deter President Saddam Hussein from further aggression, while convincing him of the allied determination to see him draw his forces back from Kuwait.

Diplomacy

There was a frantic diplomatic effort by the leaders of many countries, aimed at finding a face-saving solution that would enable President Saddam Hussein to withdraw his troops from Kuwait without acknowledging defeat. The Arab League was split over the crisis. With twelve members backing the alliance, and others neutral or leaning toward Saddam Hussein, it

West to east: U.S. troops disembark from a giant transport plane to join Operation Desert Shield in Saudi Arabia. ▶

was no longer able to make decisions. In early September the League's long-standing secretary-general, Chadli Klibi, offered his resignation. King Hussein of Jordan, who said he maintained a neutral position on the crisis, traveled widely in the Arab world and in the West, while also staying in close touch with President Saddam Hussein, looking for a diplomatic solution.

The chairman of the PLO, Yasser Arafat, had aligned himself closely with Saddam Hussein from the start, as the Palestinians in the territories occupied by Israel and elsewhere applauded Iraq's actions. But according to Palestinian sources, he also tried hard to persuade Saddam Hussein to find a way of backing down without losing face.

Non-Arab politicians also put in their best efforts: President Gorbachev of the Soviet Union and President Mitterrand of France were particularly active in the search for a peaceful solution.

The U.S. administration, together with its Arab and Western allies, was making it clear that if Iraq would not withdraw its troops, there could be no compromise. The alliance that President Bush was now skillfully holding together included many countries, but the principal partners were Britain and France, while Saudi Arabia, Egypt, and Syria were the key Arab participants. Syria was a surprising partner for the United States to work with. President Assad of Syria has long been suspected of providing funds and a haven for terrorist groups, and his stance over twenty-five years has been rigidly anti-Western. But President Assad is a rival and enemy of Saddam Hussein, and both Syria and Egypt must have hoped they would be rewarded by the United States for supporting the alliance.

Occupied Kuwait

Inside Kuwait, as time went on, the civilian population was less well treated, and suspected

◄ *Saddam Hussein loses an ally: President Bush (right) shakes hands with President Gorbachev of the Soviet Union at their meeting in Helsinki on September 9, 1990.*

resistance fighters were executed. Many young men were shot, some in circumstances of callous brutality. Stories of torture, murder, and other forms of atrocity began to emerge from Kuwait. Much physical damage was being done to the country. Iraqis systematically shipped home equipment and movable goods (hospital equipment, computers, generators) from Kuwait, and much private property (TVs, stereo systems, clothes) was looted by soldiers.

The Helsinki Summit

A key development was the Helsinki summit, when President Bush met Soviet President Gorbachev in the capital city of Finland, on September 9. The U.S. and Soviet leaders agreed to a joint statement saying that if "present measures" did not succeed, then other ways of persuading Iraq to leave would be looked at. The agreement made it clear that there would be no help forthcoming for Iraq from Moscow. There were hundreds of Soviet military technicians in Iraq, as well as thousands of Soviet citizens, but the Soviet leadership made it clear that the Soviets in Iraq would not assist the Iraqis and would be progressively withdrawn.

The summit meeting in Helsinki was widely seen as a demonstration that the deadlock in relations between the Soviet Union and the West, known as the "Cold War," was really at an end. Former Soviet leaders would almost certainly have backed President Saddam Hussein, not because of any particular belief in his ideals, but because it would have been a way of frustrating the plans of the West. In the same way, Western foreign policy for years had been centered around the idea of excluding Soviet influence from disputed regions of the world.

Israel, Iraq, and the Palestinians

Meanwhile, developments in the crisis were beginning to cause serious concern in Israel, which had for some years identified Saddam Hussein's Iraq as one of its chief enemies in the region. Part of President Saddam Hussein's

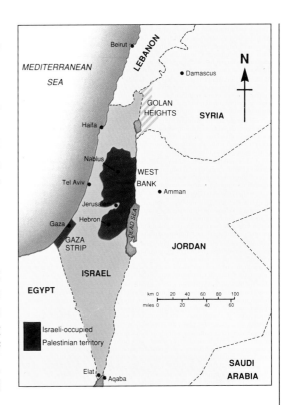

attempt to become accepted as the leader of the Arab world was to pose as the leader who would defeat Israel. Israel is a predominantly Jewish nation, which since it was founded, in 1948, had been three times at war with its Arab neighbors. In 1967, Israel invaded and occupied Palestinian Arab territories. Israel was not forced to give back the territories, despite U.N. resolutions condemning the occupation. Israel claimed that the territories were essential for its security. Now Saddam Hussein threatened that he would attack Israel if Iraq or Iraqi forces were attacked, and he put himself forward as the champion of the Palestinians. Israel reacted with military preparations and the promise that if Iraqi troops entered Jordan, whose territory lies between Iraq and Israel, Israel would feel free to retaliate.

Throughout this period President Saddam Hussein continued to link the invasion of Kuwait with the Israeli–Palestinian issue. He proposed that any possible peace talks must include negotiations over the future of the Palestinian territories occupied by Israel. The alliance consistently rejected such "linkage" between talks on Israel and Iraqi withdrawal from Kuwait.

Up to the Deadline

November, December, January

As the weeks passed, negotiations became more urgent and the likelihood that the crisis over Kuwait would end in war became more real. In the last weeks of October, President Gorbachev's envoy, Yevgeni Primakov, visited Iraq, France, the United States, Britain, Egypt, Syria, and Saudi Arabia in a punishing diplomatic tour. The Soviet negotiator was looking for any shred of compromise that might be found, even at this late stage, to get the Iraqis out of Kuwait without fighting and ward off the war that was beginning to seem inevitable. King Hussein of

Jordan and his brother Crown Prince Hassan also continued a ceaseless round of visits and talks with the same aim.

Change of Strategy

Meanwhile, intelligence assessments suggested that it would be a year before sanctions would really begin to hit Iraq and that the country was more resilient than had been estimated. This posed a serious dilemma for the alliance, because many people felt that a year was simply too long to wait while Kuwaitis

Increasing the allied military presence: U.S. troops move out into the Saudi Arabian desert in November. ▼

were suffering under the harsh conditions of the Iraqi occupation. President Bush's advisers urged him to prepare for military action. As early as mid-October, the U.S. administration decided on the basic strategy of an air campaign against Iraq beginning in mid-January, followed by a ground assault. Some people have claimed that the decision to oust the Iraqis by force was a political one, pointing out that the military experts were in favor of giving sanctions longer to work.

The U.S. Raises the Stakes

On November 8 the United States, now effectively both Iraq's principal military adversary as well as the chief negotiator for the anti-Iraq alliance, announced that it would increase its forces in Saudi Arabia by an additional 150,000 troops, bringing the total allied force to about 500,000. Iraq's forces had, in the meantime, grown to 430,000, according to American military intelligence estimates. The increase in allied strength would bring the allied forces to a level where they could attack the Iraqi defenders in Kuwait with the strength that the military

commanders believed to be necessary for success. The decision to build up the U.S. forces marked the moment when President Bush decided that, if all attempts at persuasion failed, he would sooner or later use force to drive the Iraqis from Kuwait.

Jordan and Iraq

Jordan swung dangerously close to declaring its outright support for Iraq in mid-November. The Jordanian parliament elected a new speaker from the Muslim Brotherhood, which held a large minority of the seats. Their deputies debated whether Jordan should offer military support to Iraq.

It was at this stage that the Iraqi government threatened to set fire to the oil wells in Kuwait and to cause a deliberate ecological disaster. American officials claimed they had evidence that Kuwait's oil wells were fitted with explosive charges that the Iraqis would trigger before leaving, causing devastating fires. Iraq also renewed its threats against Israel. The government in Jerusalem, in turn, threatened Iraq with unspecified but massive reprisals.

Setting the Deadline

On November 29 the U.N. Security Council passed Resolution 678, which reaffirmed all the previous U.N. Resolutions from 660 onward. It authorized member states "to use all necessary means" (including the use of force) to make Iraq comply with the previous resolutions, and notably to withdraw from Kuwait as demanded by Resolution 660. Yemen and Cuba voted against the resolution, while China abstained, but the other twelve members of the Security Council voted for it, including the Soviet Union. James Baker, the U.S. secretary of state, described the resolution as "the most important in the history of the United Nations." The resolution set a deadline for Iraq's compliance, January 15, 1991. Iraq angrily rejected Resolution 678 as having no legal force.

Talks

On November 30 President Bush announced that he was willing to send his secretary of state, James Baker, to Baghdad for direct talks with the Iraqi leadership. The Americans proposed that Iraq's foreign minister, Tarek Aziz, visit Washington during the week beginning on December 10, while Baker should go to Baghdad on some date between December 15 and January 15, the U.N. deadline. Iraq accepted the American proposal in principle on December 1, and on December 2 Baker said that if Iraq pulled out of Kuwait it would not be attacked by U.S. forces. It began to seem as if Iraq might after all be proposing to hold talks with the United States and to pull out of Kuwait at the last moment. But an ominous sign came the following day, when Iraq tested a number of Scud missiles, the Soviet-built long-range missiles with which it was feared Iraq could deliver chemical weapons.

On December 5 James Baker told the Senate Foreign Affairs Committee in Washington that Iraq risked a sudden and massive American strike if it failed to leave Kuwait and release the Western hostages it was still holding. At this point Saddam Hussein did make a move to

U.N. Resolution 678
(November 29, 1990)

1. Demands that Iraq comply fully with Resolution 660 and all subsequent relevant Resolutions, and decides, while maintaining all its decisions, to allow Iraq one final opportunity, as a pause of goodwill to do so;

2. Authorizes member states cooperating with the government of Kuwait . . . to use all necessary means to uphold and implement Security Council Resolutions 660 and all subsequent relevant Resolutions and to restore peace and security in the area.

lessen the tension, which led some observers to think that he was now genuinely seeking a way out of the crisis. The Iraqi president announced on December 6 that he would release the Western hostages, who had been part of Iraq's "human shield" policy of keeping hostages at potential military targets. It is reported that Yasser Arafat persuaded Saddam Hussein to make this decision.

The release of hostages was sufficient to lead the United States to believe that its last-ditch offer to negotiate with Saddam Hussein might bear fruit. It took some time before an agreed date was set for a meeting between Baker and Aziz, but after much delay Iraq agreed on a meeting to take place on January 9 in Geneva. In the intervening period the European Community made a serious effort to promote a compromise between Iraq and the United States, President Chadli Benjedid of Algeria mounted his own search for a peaceful compromise, and King Hussein of Jordan once again toured European capitals.

The Baker–Aziz talks in Geneva lasted six hours, but resulted in total failure, though neither statesman would disclose either the substance of the talks or the reasons why agreement had not been reached. There was disappointment throughout the world that the American and Iraqi foreign ministers had failed to reach any kind of understanding. It was hard to believe that Saddam Hussein did not realize that Iraq faced almost certain defeat if Iraqi troops did not withdraw before the U.N. deadline.

One final attempt to negotiate was made by Javier Perez de Cuellar, the U.N. secretary-general, who went to Baghdad on January 12. He saw Tarek Aziz on that day and met Saddam Hussein the following day. Like Baker's talks in Geneva, Perez de Cuellar's initiative was fruitless, and he was in a somber mood as he admitted he had failed to make any progress. On January 14 the Iraqi parliament pledged its support for Saddam Hussein, and as the U.N. deadline approached, Iraq and the world waited for what was to follow.

A last bid for peace: U.S. secretary of state, James Baker (right), meets Iraq's foreign minister, Tarek Aziz, in Geneva on January 9. ▶

The Air War

▲ *U.S. Marine Corps F-18 fighter jets about to refuel during a sortie against Iraq.*

At about 2:00 A.M. Saudi Arabian time, on January 17, American, British, and Kuwaiti aircraft took off from bases in Saudi Arabia and from aircraft carriers in the Gulf. Their mission was to begin the campaign of air strikes against targets in Baghdad and military targets in Iraq and occupied Kuwait. This was the beginning of Operation Desert Storm, the long-planned operation to liberate Kuwait.

The early attacks on Baghdad itself were fully reported in the West. Western newspaper and television reporters were in the Iraqi capital and were able to continue reporting unhampered for some time. Pictures from Baghdad were seen on Western television screens, from the CNN news-gathering network and from other channels, and assessments of the damage were given. The selected targets in Baghdad at first seemed to be calculated to damage electricity and communications systems and to paralyze the functioning of what is a relatively modern city.

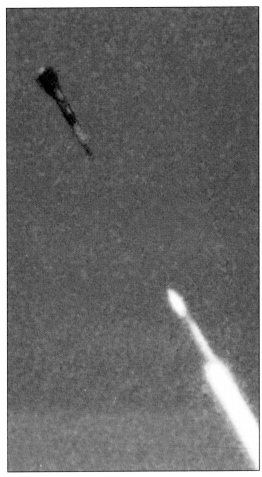

▲ January 25: Clearing up the damage in Tel Aviv, Israel, after an Iraqi Scud missile attack.

Air defenses: A Patriot missile (right) intercepts an incoming Scud. Patriot missiles proved very successful at destroying Scuds. ▶

Military briefings stressed the accuracy and "hi-tech" nature of the weapons being used by allied aircraft. Films were released showing "smart" bombs hitting targets with pinpoint accuracy, leaving adjacent buildings intact. However, most of the weapons used were in fact conventional bombs, which must have caused considerable damage around the targets at which they were aimed.

Scud Attack

Iraq soon made real its threat to extend the war to Israel, as President Saddam Hussein had said he would do if his country were attacked. The day after the beginning of the air assault on Iraq, eight Scud missiles were fired at targets in Israel. Three of these landed in Tel Aviv and one in Haifa. Another Scud was fired at the allied air base at Dhahran in Saudi Arabia. In all, thirty-nine missiles were fired at Israel during the war. One of the U.S. administration's greatest fears was that Israel would be sucked into the war, making it very difficult for the Arab members of the alliance to go on cooperating with the West.

Even though Israel's leaders made very belligerent statements, they bowed to American pressure and stayed out. One factor was that Iraq did not use chemical weapons against Israel. Iraq certainly had chemical weapons, which it had used during the Iran–Iraq war, against both Iranian forces and Iraqi Kurds. However, it may not have been able to deliver them as missile warheads. In any case it seems likely that Iraq made a political decision not to use chemical weapons. A conventional attack was sufficient to make good Saddam Hussein's claim that Iraq was in the lead in the struggle against Israel. Stories abound of Palestinians in the Occupied Territories cheering the missile attacks. But Israel had threatened massive retaliation against chemical attack, which seemed likely to mean a nuclear strike. President Saddam Hussein stopped short of bringing down such catastrophic retribution.

The Battle for Air Supremacy

Iraq's anti-aircraft defenses were active, which led to the loss of some allied aircraft, particularly on low-flying missions. Forty-two allied aircraft were lost in action. But Iraq's air force never offered much in the way of resistance to allied attacks. In retrospect, it seems as if Saddam Hussein had already decided that, as he had no chance of defeating the allies, he would conserve his air force intact for postwar use. That also offers an explanation of a phenomenon that was hard to explain at the time. Large numbers of Iraqi aircraft, reaching an eventual total of at least 136, were flown across the border to Iran, making emergency landings at small airfields and even on roads. Saddam Hussein's aim seems to have been to keep this precious resource safe from destruction by the allies.

"The Mother of All Battles"

Saddam Hussein showed no signs of backing down during the air campaign, and he constantly warned the allies and exhorted his troops to prepare for what he called "the mother of all battles." On January 30, in a surprise attack,

Iraqi forces captured the Saudi border town of Khafji and held it for more than a day. That was an operation that gave rise to speculation as to whether the Iraqis would initiate the ground fighting rather than waiting for an allied move. But it was not followed up, and it was probably intended as an all-out effort to give the allies an exaggerated impression of Iraqi morale and military readiness.

▲ *February 9: Baghdad, the main bridge over the Tigris after an allied bombing raid.*

February 16: An Iraqi newspaper, Sout Al Iraq, *reports the casualties from the allied air strike on an air raid shelter in Baghdad. The headline reads "Our people are massacred."* ▶

February 13: Iraqi emergency workers stand by bodies removed from the Baghdad air raid shelter bombed by the allies. Over 300 people were reported dead. ▼

Sout Al Iraq

صوت العراق

في هذا العدد
– من لاطفال العراق
– الشعوب المسلمة
مع ابناء العراق
–قصف المدن الآمنة
– لماذا يتعجل صدام
الحرب البرية

قال تعالى
"سبحان الذي أسرى بعبده
من المسجد الحرام الى
المسجد الاقصى الذي باركنا
حوله"

Issue 95 - 10th Year - 1991\2\16

اسلامية سياسية تصدرها طلائع الدعوة الاسلامية في اوربا

العدد ٩٥ – السنة العاشرة – ١٩٩١/٢/١٦

شعبنا يُعذّب

False Dawn

Only once, on February 15, did it seem as if the pounding Iraq and the Iraqi forces in Kuwait were receiving had brought about a change of mind. That was the day on which Iraq's Revolutionary Command Council announced that the Iraqi forces would leave Kuwait in accordance with the U.N. resolutions. That announcement gave rise to a wave of celebration in Baghdad, which incidentally demonstrated how unpopular Iraq's occupation of Kuwait had now become among the Iraqi people themselves. But it turned out to be a false hope. The promised withdrawal was hedged with unacceptable conditions, and it may only have been meant to gain a pause in the bombardment.

As the air campaign continued throughout the rest of January and much of February, misgivings began to grow among reporters and in the Western countries about the extent of the civilian casualties inflicted. People began to question the necessity of destroying so many of the amenities necessary for civilian as well as military activities in Baghdad. There was no way of assessing damage to civilian targets elsewhere in Iraq, since reporters were concentrated in the capital.

The counter argument by the political and military establishment that planned and ran the campaign was that Iraq's resources had to be destroyed to prevent reinforcements and support being given to the Iraqi troops at the front. Their argument was that the air campaign was not excessive and that it was necessary to produce demoralization among the front-line troops and to minimize allied casualties when the land war was eventually begun. Iraqi opposition figures in exile in Western countries, who had up to then supported the United States and the allied stand against President Saddam Hussein, were very uneasy. They argued that it was not necessary to destroy the country in order to dislodge the president and leave the way open for a democratic postwar Iraq, as well as a liberated Kuwait.

Oil Slick

One controversial event during the air campaign was a massive leak of oil from a Kuwaiti terminal into the Gulf, starting on January 25. It is still not clear what caused the leak. Saddam Hussein accused the allies of starting it in order to drain the fuel available to him; the allies accused Iraq of causing it so that the oil would wreck the water supply to the other Gulf states. A U.S. air strike on the terminal stopped the leak, but by then it had formed the largest oil slick the world has ever seen, causing the death of thousands of seabirds and marine life. Damage to the water supply in the Gulf states was prevented by using booms to stop the oil from getting into the water desalination plants.

The Effects of the Bombardment

The air war continued unabated until the ground assault finally began, on February 24. The total number of sorties — that is to say, individual missions — flown by allied pilots since the beginning of the war was by this time 94,000. The number of sorties flown was to reach 110,000 by the end of hostilities.

The damage sustained by Iraq was immense. Estimates of the cost to Iraq of reconstruction suggest a figure of around $110 billion. In other words, each allied sortie caused Iraq about $1 million worth of damage. The number of civilian casualties is very hard to estimate. The allies are not in a position to do more than guess and would in any case be inclined to play the figure down. Iraq has also tended to minimize the casualty figures to which it admits, in order not to concede the scale of the defeat it has suffered. Various guesses have been made, ranging up to 100,000 deaths, but this was a topic on which the allies released no intelligence information. Control of information by the allies was a subject of increasing concern and frustration for the Western press as the campaign developed. The allied aim, however, was to reduce Iraq's ability to resist by inflicting massive damage both on Iraq's armed forces and on the country that sustained them. That aim was certainly achieved.

▲ *The allied commanding officer, General Norman Schwarzkopf, at a press conference explaining how a pinpoint air strike closed off the oil leak that had caused a massive oil slick in the Gulf.*

The Land War

▲ *Allied soldiers take cover after throwing phosphorous grenades into an Iraqi trench.*

The Last Deadline

On February 20 the allied commander, American General Norman Schwarzkopf, said that he believed the Iraqi forces were on the verge of collapse, as they had been under an intensive bombardment for days. On February 22 President Bush responded to a Soviet proposal aimed at getting Iraq out of Kuwait and out of the war without battle being joined. The suggestion was that the Soviet Union would provide guarantees for Iraq's security if it would pull out of Kuwait at once and unconditionally. The Americans refused to give Iraq a pause in the bombing to arrange for a withdrawal, but did agree that if an unambiguous Iraqi withdrawal began by 8:00 P.M. that day hostilities could end. There was no sign of Iraqi withdrawal, but the Iraqis were beginning to put into action their threat to set fire to Kuwait's oil wells. By this time nothing stood in the way of the land operation, and there were increasing reasons to begin. Western critics of allied policy were starting to complain that prolonging the bombing campaign was now only causing unnecessary loss of life.

The Final Battle Lines

By the time the U.N. deadline expired on January 15 the allied forces had reached a figure of 550,000 men and women under arms in the theater of war, and more were still arriving. Some 350,000 of these troops were American, and 200,000 belonged to the various Arab and Western allied forces. These included 25,000 British troops. Iraq had an estimated 600,000 men facing them. The allies had almost 4,000 tanks, and the Iraqis more than 4,000. The impending battle, involving armies totaling well over a million, was potentially one of the largest military operations ever undertaken.

The Attack

The allied land offensive began at 4:00 A.M. Middle Eastern time on February 24, with a U.S. Marine attack on the Kuwaiti border town of el-Wafra and a rapid advance up the coast road. But the main attack was to the west, where U.S. and French forces pushed directly into Iraq, bypassing Kuwait. Their aim was to attack Iraqi forces in the rear, especially the Republican Guard, which was Saddam Hussein's élite force, and to cut off communications between Iraq and Kuwait. These were highly mobile troops and their advance was very rapid.

The initial attack was followed up by British and Arab forces. Other Arab forces were committed to the direct assault on Kuwait, together with American troops, where the allied forces fought their way north through blazing oilfields. By the end of the first day of the ground war, 200 of Kuwait's 1,000 oil wells were set on fire by retreating Iraqis. By the end of the action some 550 oil wells were on fire.

President Saddam Hussein broadcast a speech on Baghdad Radio claiming that the Iraqi army was resisting the allied attack. Iraq, he said, was poised on the brink of a great victory. In reality, the Iraqis offered virtually no resistance, and many surrendered. Probably more would have laid down their arms but for the practical difficulty of surrendering to a hostile force on the battlefield (it may be impossible to show the enemy that you want to surrender, and you may be shot by your own side for

▲ One of more than 4,000 Iraqi tanks destroyed during the swift allied advance.

desertion). Those who did not surrender attempted to flee, but the work of setting fire to the oil wells, which had been previously fitted with explosive charges, continued as the troops moved out. There were also reports of random destruction, and some Kuwaiti civilians were killed by the fleeing Iraqi soldiers.

The allied land assault continued on February 25, with the surrender of yet more Iraqi forces. The advance inside Iraq continued, and the allied hold on Kuwait was strengthened. Though Iraq did not show much resistance on the ground, a Scud missile attack on the U.S. base at Dhahran in Saudi Arabia hit a barracks and killed twenty-eight Americans.

On February 26 U.S., Saudi, and Kuwaiti troops were starting to reoccupy Kuwait City.

On the next day, as allied forces closed in on the Republican Guard positions near Basra, the principal city of southern Iraq, Saddam Hussein called for a cease-fire and offered to abandon all his claims to Kuwait. This was rejected by President Bush, and the allied attack on the Iraqi forces continued. Inside Kuwait, the allied forces finally captured Kuwait airport, where an unusually stubborn Iraqi force had held out for two days.

Cease-fire

By midnight on February 27 Iraq's forces in Kuwait had largely been destroyed, dispersed, or captured. Most of Iraq's forces were in full flight by this time, and large numbers of vehicles were destroyed and soldiers killed as allied

Iraqi troops surrender. The man in the foreground holds up his Koran to show his peaceful intent. ▼

aircraft flew strike after strike at the fleeing Iraqi troops. One huge Iraqi convoy was trapped in an enormous traffic jam on the road north from Kuwait City and became a sitting target for U.S. bombers. The continuing carnage as the Iraqis were attacked began to attract criticism for humanitarian reasons. Then, at 8:00 A.M. Middle Eastern time on February 28, just 100 hours after the ground war began, President Bush ordered a cease-fire and the hostilities ended.

Allied casualties in the campaign were very light. The coalition countries lost 139 servicemen as the result of enemy action, and an additional 56 were missing in action. By contrast, the Iraqi losses in men and equipment are almost incalculable. Tens of thousands of Iraqi troops must have been killed, and at the end of the war

there were at least 80,000 Iraqi prisoners of war in allied camps.

Iraq offered its surrender and brought the fighting definitively to an end on March 3, when Iraqi commanders met General Schwarzkopf and the allied command at a ceremony at Safwan in southern Iraq. All the allied terms for making the cease-fire permanent were accepted by the Iraqis.

On April 3 the U.N. Security Council passed Resolution 687, which formally brought the Gulf War to an end, imposing conditions on Iraq that Saddam Hussein accepted. Now that the allies had achieved their objective of driving the Iraqi forces from Kuwait, there remained the difficult and slow process of trying to build a lasting peace in the region.

▲ *Liberated Kuwaitis celebrate the arrival of allied troops in Kuwait City on February 26.*

The Land Campaign

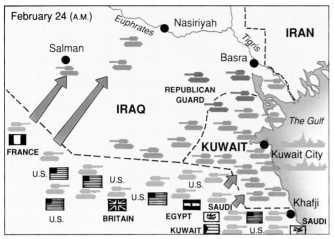

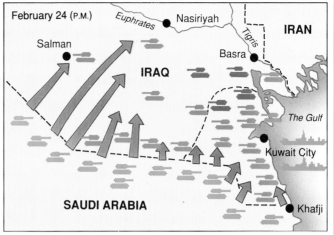

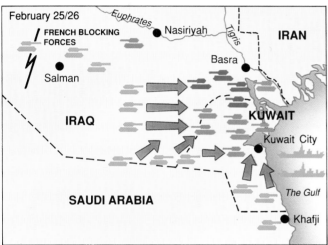

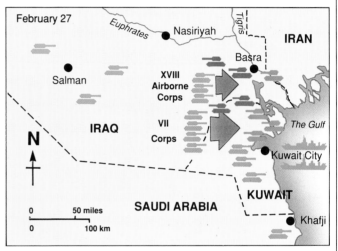

▲ *February 24 A. M.: U.S. Marines and Saudi task forces attack across the east end of the Kuwait–Saudi Arabia border while the naval forces make as if to launch an amphibious assault directly at Kuwait City. In the west, French and U.S. forces launch an overland attack to Salman airfield.*

February 24 P. M.: U.S. Marines and Saudi forces make rapid progress in the east, having breached Iraqi defenses. Egyptian and Saudi forces also launch attacks in the east. VII Corps attacks north into Iraq, west of Iraq–Kuwait border. (VII Corps consists of three U.S. armored divisions, one U.S. infantry division, and one British armored division.)

February 25/26: U.S. Marines, Saudis, and Egyptians close on Kuwait City. U.S. 24th Infantry Division cuts off Iraqi escape route north out of Kuwait. The allied force that had attacked Iraq directly veers east into Kuwait. By evening February 26, 21 Iraqi divisions rendered ineffective.

February 27: Allied forces close in on remaining Iraqi forces in Kuwait, including élite Republican Guard forces. U.S. Marines, Saudis, and Kuwaitis clear Kuwait City of remaining Iraqi resistance.

U.N. Resolution 687 (Principal Conditions)

Cease-fire: The cease-fire comes into effect when Iraq accepts the resolution.

Borders: Iraq and Kuwait must respect the disputed border, which will be demarcated by the U.N. The Security Council will guarantee the frontier.

Disarmament: Iraq must accept the destruction or removal of all chemical and biological weapons and ballistic missiles with ranges greater than 90 miles. A similar procedure applies to nuclear material. The U.N. will monitor and verify destruction and removal.

Compensation: Iraq is liable for damages arising from its invasion of Kuwait payable out of its oil revenues.

Sanctions: The embargo on food is removed. Other sanctions will be lifted after weapons are removed. An arms embargo is maintained.

The Future of the Gulf

The principal question asked after the war was whether one of the results of the conflict would be greater democracy for the people of the Gulf. Saudi Arabia has been run as an autocracy by the Saudi ruling family since the foundation of the state and its full international recognition in 1932. Democracy remained out of the question, but the Saudi government had been considering the establishment of an appointed "consultative council" for some time. The war has opened Saudi eyes to the possibilities of change, and as the allied forces left they were already considering some way of providing expression for public opinion.

In Kuwait the first priority was to restore law and order. A grave problem was presented by Kuwaiti citizens settling private scores. Many Palestinians, Sudanese, and Yemenis, and others who were thought to have favored Saddam Hussein, have suffered at the hands of angry Kuwaitis. This presented an excuse for the emir, Jaber al-Sabah, to defer the reintroduction of Kuwait's democratic constitution until questions of public order and reconstruction have been settled.

The cost of the damage to Kuwait has been estimated at about $30 billion. With the damage to the oilfields, as well as the loss in value of Kuwait's foreign investments, it was clear that Kuwait was permanently changed. Kuwait's opposition politicians were demanding the restoration of the democratic constitution, and the ruling family's arguments for refusing were beginning to seem less than convincing.

Environmental Effects

The ecological damage caused by oil spillages may damage the Gulf fishing industry, not to mention the harm done to marine wildlife as a whole. The effects of the burning oil wells could have even greater consequences. Deadly pollution was being caused in Kuwait itself, and black rain and snow — caused when the clouds precipitate — had been reported as far away as Pakistan and the Soviet Union. It can only be guessed what harm the burning wells have done to Kuwait's oil resources.

Gulf Security

It looked probable in the postwar period that the Gulf Cooperation Council would be resuscitated with U.S. assistance. The United States was looking for some way to provide permanent security for the Gulf states, without a large-scale or permanent U.S. presence in the region. Cooperation with the GCC, together with agreed arrangements for the rapid transfer of American troops if another threat should arise, looked likely to provide the necessary safeguard for the Gulf region and to serve what the United States saw as its legitimate interest in insuring the supply of oil.

The expensive and difficult process of trying to put out the burning Kuwaiti oil wells. ▼

Meanwhile the Gulf states also signed the agreement known as the Damascus Charter with the Arabs who had been their allies. The Charter provides for economic help for Egypt and Syria from the Gulf, in return for Syrian and Egyptian military backing for the GCC states. As well as receiving payments from the Gulf states, Egypt had a debt of $7 billion owed to the United States canceled, and Syria has received more than $2 billion in payments from Saudi Arabia.

Elsewhere in the Arab world, states such as Jordan and Tunisia, which had come close to offering explicit support to Iraq, were quickly mending their fences with alliance countries such as Egypt. Tunisian President Ben Ali visited Egypt, and Jordan's King Hussein appeared on television immediately after the cease-fire to ask the rest of the Arab world to understand why Jordan had acted as it had and to forget and forgive. Though it might be some time before the Arab League would attempt to hold another summit meeting, ministerial meetings were soon being held at the Arab League's headquarters in Cairo.

Iraq: Continued Instability

In Iraq itself, the postwar period started a phase of upheaval inside the country. President Bush called on the Iraqi people to overthrow President Saddam Hussein: "We are not targeting Saddam, but I've already said that the Iraqi people should put him aside." But the United States did not provide military support for the rebels. It seems possible that the United States was encouraging a military coup within the Iraqi leadership. The Kurds in the north and the Shi'ites in the south rose up against Saddam Hussein's government. They were promptly crushed by the armed forces left to Saddam Hussein after the war. Hundreds of thousands of Kurds fled to Turkey and Iran, but found themselves without food, water, or shelter. Aid did eventually arrive, and U.N.-sanctioned "safe havens," protected by allied forces, were set up for the Kurds in northern Iraq, with the agreement of the Iraqi government.

Saddam Hussein promised some concessions. He said the Kurds would have autonomy, and he promised the abolition of the ruling Revolutionary Command Council, handing power instead to the ministers and the national assembly. The costs of the war were enormous, at an estimated $110 billion worth of damage and lost income. These costs came on top of those of the Iran–Iraq War, which amounted to some $500 billion.

Israel

Soon after the war, the U.S. secretary of state, James Baker, started a series of talks with Israel, Jordan, the Palestinians, and Syria over the Palestinian and Syrian territories occupied by Israel. Israel's government has been determined to seek peace on its own terms, which was increasingly coming to mean keeping the Occupied Territories while giving their inhabitants limited autonomy. This was not acceptable to the Palestinians or the Arab states, so a lasting peaceful settlement seems some way off.

The Role of the U.N.

Some have argued that the construction of the international alliance against Iraq and the use of U.N. resolutions were both smokescreens to disguise an American action in defense of its own interests. This was the view of those countries from the developing world within the Security Council during the war: Yemen, Cuba, Malaysia, and Colombia. Yemen and Cuba voted against most of the resolutions that enabled the United States to prosecute the war, or at least abstained. It was argued that without opposition from the Soviet Union, the United States found it easy to dominate the Security Council. In particular, Secretary-General Perez de Cuellar was thought not to have kept a sufficiently high profile during the crisis.

On the other hand, many saw the U.N. involvement in the Gulf War as a model for solving future conflicts: Iraq had broken international law, and, despite having a massive army, it had been made to obey international law by forces the U.N. itself had sanctioned.

New World Order?

With the coming of the new era of good relations between the United States and the Soviet Union, President Bush had said he looked forward to a "new world order." Instead of politics being dominated by the two superpowers fighting each other, their efforts could be combined in upholding international law and promoting peace. The Gulf crisis offered the first real test of this theory, and indeed the agreement between Presidents Gorbachev and Bush at the crucial Helsinki summit in September 1990 certainly seemed to offer a new direction in world politics. It seemed as if the countries of the world could now act together to punish states that broke international law. But it could also be argued that the war did not bring the underlying conflict to an end. The confrontation between those Arab states with larger populations and relatively less wealth ranged against the wealthy Gulf states is still there. Tension will remain until the problems of social and economic deprivation and inequality in the Arab world begin to be resolved.

For world security, the lesson may be that the United States, now effectively the world's only superpower, can settle international conflicts according to its own wishes, acting as an international police force. The U.N. will be able to exercise some moral control but little practical restraint. However, the United States' power is tempered by the immense cost of such operations (the Gulf War is thought to have cost the allies $70 billion), as well as the dangerous political upheavals they cause, not to mention the human suffering. But perhaps the most sober reflection is that the war between the United States and Iraq, coming after the end of the old confrontation between East and West, may have been the first war between North and South, between the developed world and the less developed, over the question of who controls the world's dwindling resources.

◀ *Kurdish refugees struggle for bread at a makeshift camp on the Turkish border. The Kurds fled from Northern Iraq after the brief but bloody civil war that followed Iraq's defeat by the allies.*

Glossary

ACC

The Arab Cooperation Council was formed in 1989 by Iraq, Jordan, North Yemen (Yemen Arab Republic), and Egypt. South Yemen (People's Democratic Republic of Yemen) and North Yemen merged in 1990. Its purpose was economic, political, and military cooperation. Its inaugural meeting was in Baghdad, and President Saddam Hussein saw it as a vehicle for extending his influence. The Gulf War and Egypt's opposition to Iraq rendered it inoperative.

Autocracy

The word autocracy commonly refers to a dictatorial style of government that ignores internal opposition or dissent.

Autonomy

Autonomy means self-government, and it is commonly used to refer to forms of self-government that stop short of full statehood.

Baath party

The Baath is the ruling party of both Iraq and Syria, though the two Baath parties of these two countries are opposed to each other. The idea of the Baath, which means "rebirth" or "resurrection," is the fulfillment of the Arab people, in one country without frontiers, organized according to socialist and egalitarian principles. The Baath was founded by a Syrian Christian, Michel Aflaq, during World War II.

Embargo

A trade embargo is the prohibition of trade with a certain country or in certain commodities or goods.

Expatriate

An expatriate is a person who lives or works outside his or her own country by choice, without relinquishing his or her original nationality.

GCC

The Gulf Cooperation Council is a political, economic, and military alliance of the Gulf states, established in 1981. Its members are Bahrain, Kuwait, Oman, Qatar, Saudi Arabia, and the United Arab Emirates. Its stated aim is the defense of the Gulf against external threats — such as Iraq's invasion of Kuwait.

GNP

GNP, or gross national product, is an economic term that means the total value of the goods and services produced in a country in a year. GNP per head, or GNP divided by the number of people in the country, is a useful measure of wealth. GNP is generally expressed in U.S. dollars for purposes of international comparison.

Hashemite

The Hashemites were the ruling families descended from the sherif of Mecca, Hussein Ibn Ali, whose sons led the Arab revolt and became rulers in various Arab countries after World War I. The family belonged to a tribe known as the Bani Hashem. Sherif Hussein's son Faisal became ruler in Iraq, Abdullah was emir of Transjordan, and Ali was briefly king of Hejaz, before the Saudi royal family drove him out. King Hussein of Jordan, Abdullah's grandson, is the last remaining Hashemite monarch.

International law

International law governs dealings between states. There is no binding international law, but there is a body of legal precedents, or examples, built up from legal opinions issued over points of conflict between states, and from international agreements and treaties, by which most states agree to be bound. There is an international court of justice, and international law has a strong moral and customary authority.

Jihad

Jihad is an Arabic word that literally means "struggle." It is a Muslim's duty to engage in a *jihad* on behalf of Islam. This mainly takes the form of striving to improve oneself, to be a better Muslim, and to propagate the Faith. The popular sense of *jihad* is a "holy war," when it is claimed that a literal war against unbelievers, or against bad Muslims, may be in the interests of Islam. The idea of a *jihad* often alarms Westerners, just as for Muslims "crusade" is a disturbing concept.

The Koran

The Koran is the holy book of Islam, and Islam is founded on the belief that the Koran consists of the revelations given by God to the Prophet Muhammad in A.D. 610. The Koran was dictated to Muhammad in Arabic by the Angel Jibra'il, and it is regarded by Muslims as the created word of God. Its Arabic form is essential to it, and no translation is valid as more than an indication of the Koran's meaning.

Occupied Territories

The Occupied Territories is the name widely given to the Palestinian territory that was captured by Israel in the war between Israel and the Arabs in 1967. In Israel these lands are commonly called simply the "Territories," or the "Areas." The Occupied Territories comprise the West Bank and the Gaza Strip. The West Bank is an area to the west of the Jordan River and is a part of historic Palestine that was annexed by Jordan after the war of 1948. The Gaza Strip is a small area on the Mediterranean coast of Israel adjoining Sinai, which was formerly administered by Egypt.

OPEC

The Organization of Petroleum Exporting Countries, which comprises the Arab oil-exporting states and some other major exporters, was set up in 1960. Its members are Algeria, Ecuador, Gabon, Indonesia, Iran, Iraq, Kuwait, Libya, Nigeria, Qatar, Saudi Arabia, United Arab Emirates, and Venezuela. It controls 64 percent of the world's oil resources and plays a major role in setting oil prices.

Palestine

Palestine is the historical name of the territory presently comprised by Israel and the Occupied Territories. Until 1948 it was a mandated territory, administered by Great Britain on behalf of the United Nations Palestine was part of the Turkish-ruled Ottoman Empire until the British mandate was set up after World War I. The Arab inhabitants of the territory and their descendants are known as Palestinians. Many Palestinians want some part of historic Palestine to be restored to them as an independent Palestinian state.

Revolutionary Command Council

In Iraq the Revolutionary Command Council was a body composed of trusted military and civilian associates of President Saddam Hussein, which actually carried responsibility for running the country. Saddam Hussein promised to abolish the Revolutionary Command Council after the Gulf War.

Sovereignty

Sovereignty is one of the key concepts of international law. A sovereign state is one that is independent and regarded by other states as fully competent and within its rights to administer its own internal and external affairs. The U.N. has taken the view in the past that it is beyond its powers to interfere in the internal affairs of a sovereign state.

U.N.

The United Nations is the world body formed in 1945 after World War II with the principal aim of maintaining international peace. All sovereign states have the right of membership. All countries participate in the General Assembly, and fifteen are members of the Security Council. The United States, the Soviet Union, Britain, France, and China are permanent members of the Security Council, and the other ten seats are held in turn by states chosen from the membership of the U.N. to represent the rest of the world. Security Council resolutions may be rejected if one of the permanent members exercises its veto, but otherwise they are passed by a majority vote. These resolutions are not binding but have a strong moral force over U.N. members.

Key Events in the Crisis

August 2, 1990: 2:00 A.M. Iraqi tanks and troops invade Kuwait, taking Kuwait City. U.N. Resolution 660 condemns Iraq's invasion of Kuwait.

August 6: U.N. Resolution 661 effectively imposes trade embargo on Iraq.

August 8: Saddam Hussein announces annexation of Kuwait by Iraq.

August 10: U.N. Resolution 662 unanimously condemns Iraq's annexation of Kuwait.

August 15: Saddam Hussein agrees to all the demands made by Iran at the time of the cease-fire in the Iran–Iraq war in 1988.

August 18: Speaker of Iraq's parliament announces that Iraq would be the "host" of Westerners who had been in Kuwait and Iraq at time of invasion, effectively keeping them hostage as "human shields."

August 25: U.N. Resolution 665 allows the use of force to halt ships suspected of trading with Iraq.

August 28: Iraqi presidential decree declares Kuwait Iraq's nineteenth province.

September 1: Freed Western women and children start to leave Iraq.

September 9: Helsinki summit between U.S. President George Bush and Soviet President Mikhail Gorbachev; leaders agree on plan to deal with Iraq.

November 29: U.N. Resolution 678 authorizes member states to "use all necessary means" to make Iraq comply with previous resolutions.

December 6: Saddam Hussein announces release of Western hostages.

January 9, 1991: Talks between U.S. secretary of state, James Baker, and Iraqi foreign minister, Tarek Aziz, in Geneva fail to make any progress.

January 12: U.N. secretary general, Javier Perez de Cuellar, makes final attempt to negotiate with Saddam Hussein. Talks fail.

January 15: U.N. deadline for Iraqi withdrawal from Kuwait. Iraqi forces do not retreat.

January 17: 2:00 A.M. allied air bombardment of Iraq begins.

January 30: Iraqi forces capture Khafji and hold it for just over a day before retreating.

February 15: Iraq's Revolutionary Command Council announces that Iraqi forces would leave Kuwait in accordance with U.N. resolutions... but only on certain conditions, which are unacceptable to allies.

February 22: United States agrees that if an unambiguous Iraqi withdrawal begins by 8:00 P.M. hostilities could end. No Iraqi withdrawal.

February 24: 4:00 A.M. land attack begins.

February 27: Kuwait City liberated. Iraq's forces in Kuwait largely destroyed, dispersed, or captured.

February 28: 8:00 A.M. President Bush orders a cease-fire and hostilities end.

March 3: All the allied terms for making cease-fire permanent are accepted by Iraqis.

April 3: U.N. Resolution 687 formally ends Gulf War. Iraq accepts conditions.

Further Reading

Abdallah, Maureen S. *The Middle East.* Needham Heights, Massachusetts: Silver, Burdett & Ginn, 1986.

Evans, Michael. *The Gulf Crisis.* NY: Gloucester, 1988.

Johnson, Julia. *United Arab Emirates.* NY: Chelsea House, 1988.

Kurland, Gerald. *The Arab–Israeli Conflict.* Charlottesville, New York: SamHar Press, 1973.

Mannetti, Lisa. *Iran and Iraq: Nations at War.* NY: Franklin Watts, 1986.

Messenger, Charles. *Middle East.* NY: Franklin Watts, 1988.

Pimlott, John. *Middle East: A Background to the Conflicts.* NY: Franklin Watts/Gloucester, 1991.

Pridham, Brian. *Arab Gulf and the Arab World.* NY: Routledge, Chapman & Hall, 1988.

Ross, Stewart. *The United Nations.* NY: Franklin Watts, 1990.

Stetoff, Rebecca. *West Bank–Gaza Strip.* NY: Chelsea House, 1988.

Index